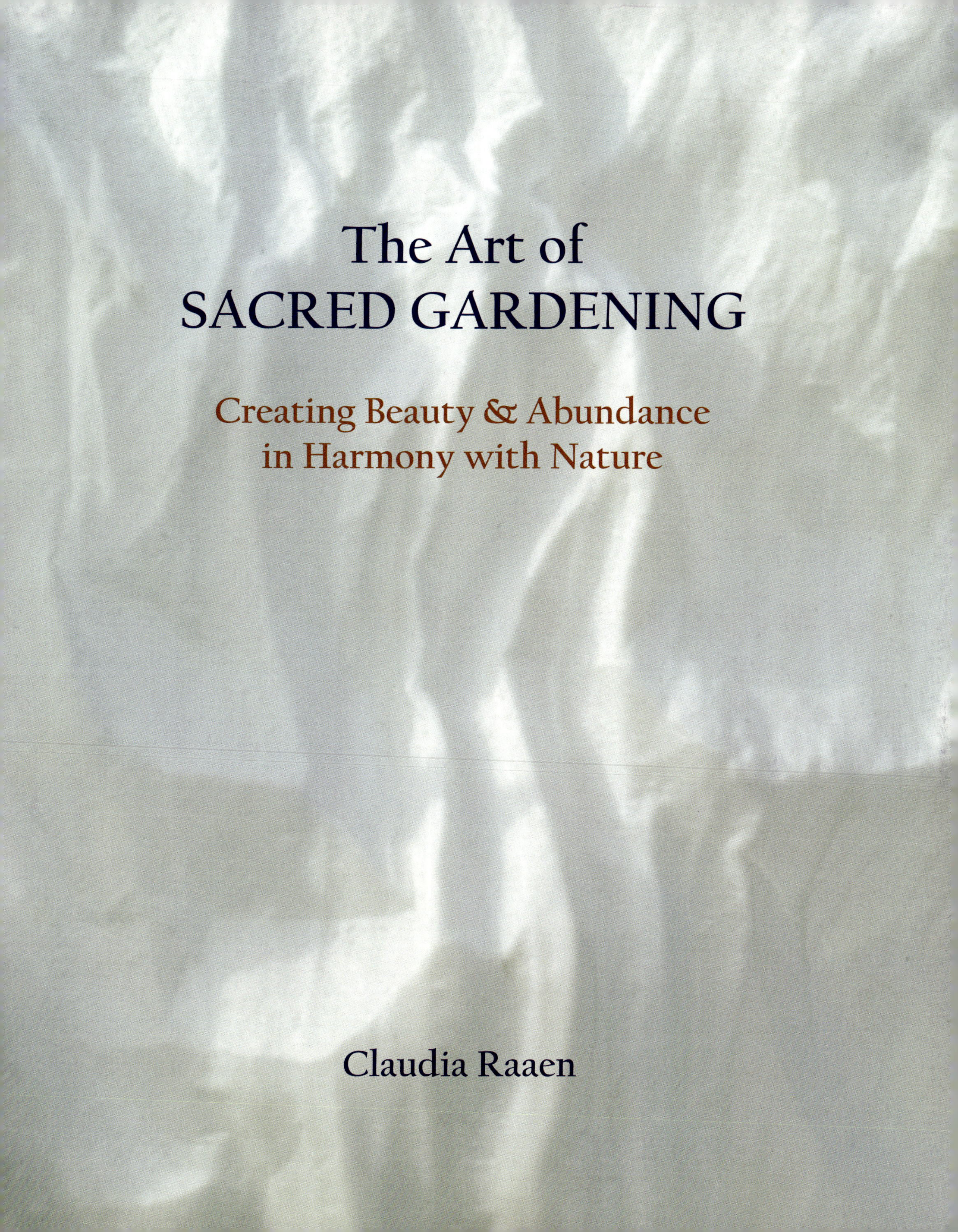

The Art of SACRED GARDENING

Creating Beauty & Abundance in Harmony with Nature

Claudia Raaen

Welcome

A Sacred Garden is
a garden of Love

My Gift to You

This book unfurls the petals of my heart, exudes the fragrance of my soul and offers up the fruits of my practice.

"My Wish"

I want you to be in Love with Mother Earth, caring for her and knowing how beautiful and abundant she is.

I want you to have a calm and quiet place to nourish your soul.

I want you to find your deepest knowing, connected to Source, and have a meaningful everyday relationship with the Divine.

I want you to know your heart's innermost treasures and believe in them.

I want you to celebrate your uniqueness and express yourself genuinely and joyfully.

I want you to be true to yourself in the purest way and return to innocence.

For myself, I want to blossom and give you the best of my Love.

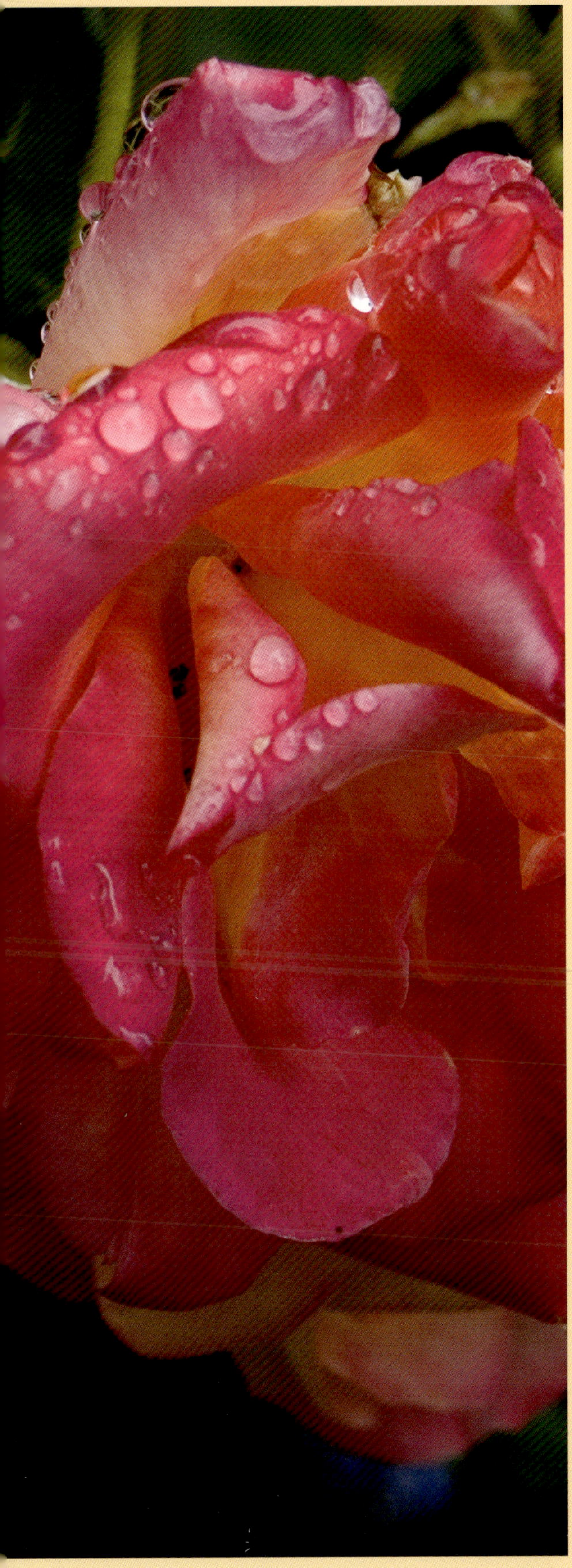

You are invited
to enter into your Heart
to create a Sacred Garden of your own.

As you journey through this book you will find exquisite views of Nature's beauty, inspiring activities for creating your Sacred Garden, and nurturing wisdom to ponder throughout your day.

Each chapter opens a gate for you to enter into the Sacred Garden. As you pass through each timeless gate you will gather meaningful experiences and helpful tools to move you confidently to the next rewarding place.

Gates & Activities

First Gate

Second Gate

Third Gate

Fourth Gate

Fifth Gate

You can dream up a Sacred Garden that is just right for *you*. It could be a small container garden spilling out with colour and fragrance, a bountiful backyard garden, a kitchen herb garden, a wild medicine garden, a self-sustaining family domain or a beautiful bed of flowers.

If making a garden is not an option for you at this time, let the contents of this book provide nourishment for your heart to blossom and fertile ground for your imagination to take root.

I suggest that you read through the whole book and let the contents percolate in your inner garden before you begin doing the activities.

Mother Earth
in her dazzling brilliance
exudes the perfect
Sacred Garden.

She provides a nest of comfort for all
where lush and tender shoots emerge,
sparkling dewdrop mirrors shine,
silky iridescent petals glow,
sweet and musky fragrances beckon,
bees hum around blossoms,
and birds splash rainwater
on their wings.

What a grand invitation
to participate and co-create!

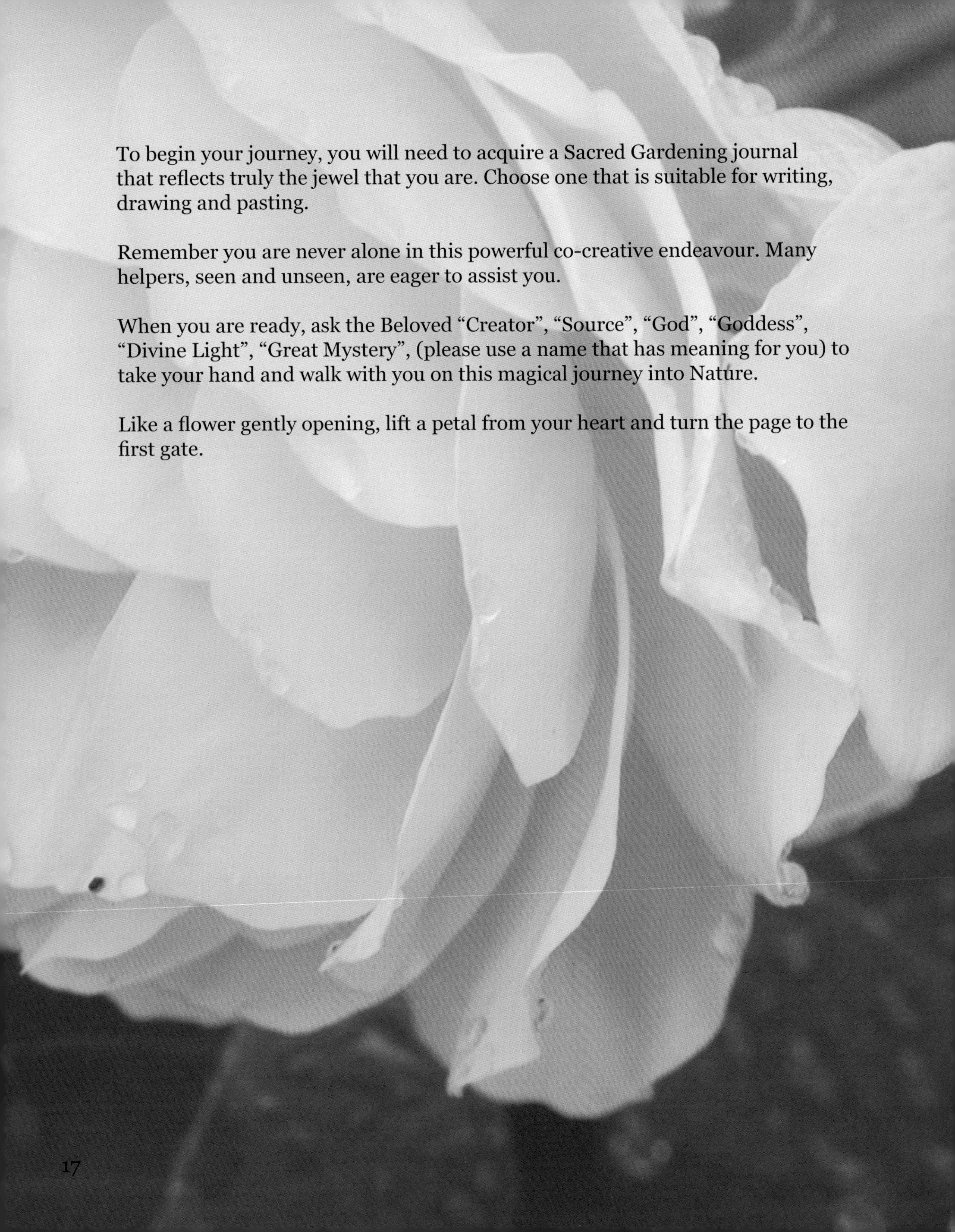

To begin your journey, you will need to acquire a Sacred Gardening journal that reflects truly the jewel that you are. Choose one that is suitable for writing, drawing and pasting.

Remember you are never alone in this powerful co-creative endeavour. Many helpers, seen and unseen, are eager to assist you.

When you are ready, ask the Beloved “Creator”, “Source”, “God”, “Goddess”, “Divine Light”, “Great Mystery”, (please use a name that has meaning for you) to take your hand and walk with you on this magical journey into Nature.

Like a flower gently opening, lift a petal from your heart and turn the page to the first gate.

First Gate

Seeding Your Intent

Within every seed exists the whole.
As you seed the intent of your Sacred Garden,
it is created within, preparing to grow.

Seeding Your Intent Activity

Connect with Your Inner Purpose

Choose a cozy, comfortable place inside or outside to have some quiet time.

Is there anything else that you need to be really comfortable? A cushion or a blanket? A drink of water?

When you are settled, gently close your eyes and simply notice that your body is breathing, for a few breaths.

Register that the body has weight and is supported by the ground or floor. This simple tool of bringing the attention of the mind to the breath and the weight of the body allows more receptivity. I do this often throughout the day.

Place your hand or hands, whichever feels more comfortable, on your heart and ask yourself honestly "What do I want, for and from, my Sacred Garden?"

Without holding anything back write down your stream of thoughts and feelings. Let it all flow out without limiting your ideas.

Now place your hand on your heart and ask the Creator (again using a word for God or Source that you relate to) if there is anything else that could be added.

Write down any new thoughts and feelings that come up. Take your time. These insights are special gifts for you so take notice.

Look over all that you have written. This is your wish list. It is the seed of your Sacred Garden. Isn't it incredible?

Read the list out loud.

Say, "Thank you Beloved, it is done."

My Story:
The moment I completed this "Seeding Your Intent" activity, after I said, "Thank you Beloved, it is done" I was startled by an eagle swooping down just in front of me. Then a friend walked up and offered me freshly baked chocolate chip cookies, plus she offered to help out in my garden. These are the signs of confirmation to notice!

Message #1
Pay attention to the signs,
confirmation from the Divine.

Second Gate

Your Inner Attitude Conditions The Soil

Your inner attitude affects every particle of your Sacred Garden.

Cultivate the four key attitudes of:

Gratitude

Honesty

Simplicity

Sincerity

Gratitude

If you catch yourself complaining about something, you have an opportunity.

As soon as you see the complaint in your mind, accept it for what it is. Then ask yourself, "What can I be grateful for in this moment?" There is always something.

Shifting from complaining into gratitude will transform you and your garden into a happier place.

Honesty

How often do you ask yourself, “Is this what I truly want or value?” Sometimes there is a hidden agenda deep down inside. See if you can find one!

Be honest with yourself.

What is motivating you? What is it? Ponder these kinds of questions while you tend your garden.

Do you ever catch yourself saying things you don’t really mean? Or perhaps using habitual language like “this always happens” or “whatever!”?

See if you can express yourself more authentically.

Honesty will set you free and put you on track where you want to be.

Simplicity

Why is the mind always making things so complicated?

Keep it simple. Simple is good.

Ask Good Creator, “How can this design, task or creation be made more simple?”

Let go of extra.

Look to Nature for a mirror of simplicity.

Sincerity

Be in your heart.

Let go of pressures that are coming from the outside. Be honest with your real feelings.

Take a deeper look beneath the surface of your mind. If you find yourself saying "I should do that", who is telling you? Do you agree with that voice? Ask yourself, "Is that true to what I value or know?" If it is, then do the task willingly. If it isn't true, then let it go.

Be true to your heart and stand up for what you value.

When you tend your inner garden with loving care and integrity, your outer garden blossoms brilliantly.

My Story:
One time when I did this "Gratitude" activity, first I noticed the heavy grey clouds began to lift off the ocean horizon, exposing blue sky and snowcapped mountains. How exciting! Then gusts of wind arrived with raven and crow swooping and playing above me. I listened to their amazing calls. Colours seemed to get more vivid and sharp. Because it was winter, I didn't see any flowers in the garden, but after I gave thanks, I turned to stand up and there greeting me was a shining orange calendula flower. When we give our loving attention to Nature, mutual blessings are exchanged.

Gratitude Activity

Develop Your Relationship with Nature by Giving and Receiving Presence

Skip into your garden or special spot in Nature. Bring your journal with you.

Find a comfortable sitting position. Notice that your body is breathing and has weight on the ground.

Look around and begin to appreciate the beauty that you see in Nature, without focusing much on one thing. Be sure to look up at the sky and down at the ground.

Soften inside, feeling your heart and say, "Thank you Divine Creator" giving your gratitude.

Letting go of expectations, notice what is happening around you. What life is showing up? Notice changes in weather, sounds, animals, insects or people. Tune into them.

Watch and listen for at least ten minutes as you continue to emanate more gratitude and appreciation.

If judgment, doubt, or rationalizations come into your mind, let them pass by like a breeze. Allow wonder to arise.

When you feel ready, give thanks for your exchange with Life. Record your experience in your journal.

Message #2

Gratitude

is nourishment for life.

THIRD GATE

Ask and Receive Before You Sow the Seed

Communication with the Divine
opens the door of heaven on Earth.

My very old and wise dear friend reminds me, “You have to ask”.
Why is something so simple and obvious difficult to put into practice?

Do you find yourself rushing ahead to do something important without taking a moment? When you work in your garden ask the Divine Creator and Nature to assist you and co-create with you. If questions arise, then ask to be shown in a way that you will understand.

Cultivate beginner's mind.

Be open to new ideas about life.

In order to receive, we must practice being receptive, giving ourselves to the moment.

Bringing the attention of the mind to the breath and the activity of the body is a quick and effective way to become more receptive.

Knock Three Times Activity

Open to Your Intuitive Nature

Are you ready to jump into Nature's magical kingdom with a childlike sense of wonder?

Bring yourself to one of your favourite places in Nature. It must have at least one tree.

Look around and pick out a tree that most draws your attention. Walk up to it, acknowledge it, appreciate its beauty and knock three times on it. Ask the Divine and Nature, to enter the kingdom. Remember to say "please" and "thank you". Put your ear to the tree and listen.

Now go exploring. Ask to be guided along the way.

Listen for your intuitive knowing. Be open to new ways of seeing and communication. If anything interesting crosses your path or shows up, pay attention. Nature has a sign language. Let it be revealed to you.

Notice your thoughts. If they inspire you, pay attention. If they are judgmental, accept that fact, and let them pass.

Allow some spontaneity on your journey. Listen for any personal messages.

When your adventure feels complete, knock three times again on a tree and give thanks for the gifts you have received.

Be sure to write them in your journal.

Message #3

You need to get off the beaten path. Explore where you haven't been before.

Choosing a Sacred Garden Site Activity

Attune to Your Environment

This activity is fun and helpful even if you already have a garden.

Think of where you would like your garden to be or where it already is and go there. Remember to bring your journal along.

Take your time getting comfortable and quiet inside. Notice your body is breathing and has weight.

Take a moment to reflect on the four inner attitudes of gratitude, honesty, simplicity and sincerity. Allow yourself to feel gratitude for all that is around you.

From your heart, ask Divine Creator and Nature if this is a good site for your Sacred Garden.

Let the communication come through feelings, thoughts and ideas. Don't get too attached to anything yet. This is a process.

Could this site provide the basic needs for your Sacred Garden, such as appropriate soil, light, water and protection from wind?

Is it a place that you would easily spend time in? Take your time noticing.

Ask if there is another site that would be good to consider.

If you are inquiring about an existing garden, ask if shifting it slightly or sizing it differently would be beneficial.

Let the ideas and feelings come as you open to possibilities. Begin to write these thoughts and feelings in your journal.

You may have some clarity at this stage, or not. It doesn't matter. Give thanks and say "It is done. Show me the way."

When the time is right to begin your garden, you can simply make a choice for your site and trust in this co-creative process. There is so much to discover and learn!

Message #4

Treat every garden as a Sacred Garden.

Fourth Gate

Declaring Sacred Space Within & Without

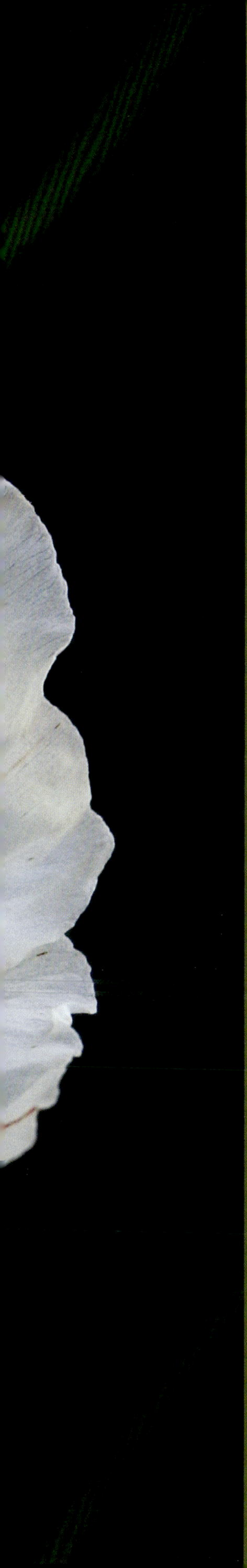

Declaring Sacred Space is setting your intention to invite the Highest Good.

It is a purification.

In order to create Sacred Space one must clean up and clear out any clutter inside and outside to make space for the new.

Like attracts like. Flow invites harmony.

Your outer garden mirrors your inner life.

How about a spring clean?

Declaring Sacred Space Activity

Purify Through Intent

This simple activity is powerful and significant.

Part I: Within

Find a quiet place where you will not be interrupted.

Close your eyes and notice your body is breathing. See if you could be more comfortable.

Bring your awareness to your inner heart space.

Say, "I declare Sacred Space within. It is done. Now and forever. Divine Creator restore me to my trueness."

Stay focused on your inner heart space and witness what is happening until the process feels complete.

Say, "Thank you, it is done."

Over the next few hours, days or even weeks if you experience an increase in negative thoughts or feelings, know that you are purifying and allow them to pass.

Drink plenty of clean water, be gentle with yourself, and remember to ask for help when you need it.

Write about your experience in your journal.

Part II: For the Garden

Go to your garden site or existing garden.

Look around and walk to the spot that you feel gives you the most power.
Don't think about it just let your body bring you there.

When you find it, notice your body breathing for three full breaths.

Say with authority, "I declare this garden Sacred Space. It is done.
Now and forever. Thank you Divine Creator. Show me the way."

Notice what happens inside and out.

When you are ready, write about your experiences.

Declaring Sacred Space clears the way for your Sacred Garden to manifest.
And so it is.

Now that you have stated your intention and asked for guidance, when you get a nudge to do something, follow your intuition and do it.

Message #5

Claim authority of your space.

Now that you have declared your garden sacred, it's time to take a closer look.

Give Nature a place in your garden to express its wild order.

When you listen to the rhythms of Nature
and follow the music of the Divine,
a harmonious dance unfolds.

Seeing the Wild Places Activity

Learn to See Nature's Order

Go on a visit to your garden site or existing garden. If your site is completely bare, then go to the nearest wilder spot. Bring your journal with you.

Walk around the area and observe how Nature orders things. Look at the various weeds and the spacing between plants. Are they spread out or in patches? Look at size, shape, colour nuances, hair, prickles and sheen. Take your time.

Which ones like to soak up the sun or hide in the shade? Who are the tough ones that can grow anywhere?

Start poking around in the soil, in several different spots. Smell it, feel it through your fingers. What is it made of?

Instead of analyzing, just notice what you see. Become interested.

Look for areas that are lush, dark and green, or sandy, dry and barren.

Listen and look for signs of insect or animal life.

Check out the trees and bushes. What grows underneath them? Is the soil any different there?

How about those ancient rocks? What is their function?

Are there any surprises in all that you have seen? What do you especially like?

Write down any insights or ideas you have about your garden site.

Take a walk on the wild side.

Message #6
Before you decide what you want
in your Sacred Garden,
it's good to realize
what you already have.

Fairy Paths

Be on the lookout for Nature's subtle energy pathways. Keep these "fairy paths" clear when you see them and let Nature go about its business. The more you encourage and support Nature's helpers in and around your garden, the more of life's magic will continue to show up.

FIFTH GATE

Gathering Your Sacred Ingredients

What do you *really* want in your Sacred Garden?

Choose what your heart desires and be open to surprises.

Identifying What You Truly Want Activity

Discover What Is Uniquely You

Now it's your turn!

You can do this activity in your garden site or some place where you will be comfortable. Bring your journal.

Take a few moments to quiet your mind, notice your body breathing, and connect with your heart.

For fun and inspiration, review what you wrote during the "Seeding Your Intent Activity".

Now, imagine plants that you would love to see in your garden. Gorgeous fragrant roses, fruit trees, healing herbs, favourite vegetables, sumptuous berries, twisty shrubs, scented groundcovers, white moonlit blossoms.

The important thing is to identify your favourite kinds of plants, whether it is a few or many. If you do not know the names then describe the particulars.

Next begin writing down any features you wish to have in your garden: a quiet sitting place, a birdbath, arbours dangling with rose and clematis, elegant winding pathways, a charming swing, a gorgeous pot. Simplicity and honesty are your friends in this.

How might you water your garden? Sprinklers, drip irrigation, watering can, rain, other?

Now place your hands on your heart, close your eyes, and ask the Beloved if there is anything that you need to add to your list.

Write down anything that comes to your mind even if it seems a little unusual.

Say, "Thank you. It is done. Show me the way."

This is your special wish list.

You may want to browse garden books and catalogues or visit nurseries and gardens to gather information. Remember to stay true to what inspires you, and allow your one-of-a-kind Sacred Garden to emerge.

Message #7

Choose what you love and love what you have.

SIXTH GATE

Designing with Nature

Sacred Shapes

Have you noticed repeating shapes and patterns in flower petals and leaves, water and cloud patterns, insect markings and seeds, landscapes and body parts? Let's take a closer look at this.

MANDALAS

Mandala means mini-universe.
Everything in Nature is made of repeating shapes, connecting patterns, cycles and rhythm.

Garden Mandala

Beginning with inspiration I trust, I act, I surrender
Take shape, make repetition, forming pattern
I give, I receive, a cycle, another cycle of growth
A process unfolding, creating something unique and perfect.

Creating a Mandala Activity

Discover the Interconnection of Forms

It's time to create with cosmic shapes! As above, so below.

Choose a 'not too windy' day for this activity. Bring a gathering basket and a camera if you'd like a picture of your mandala.

Begin with a little walk in Nature.

Look closely at the signature shapes of the leaves or flowers of a plant that draws your attention.

Examine the connecting points to see how shapes and parts are joined together.

Imagine the plants as characters making gestures like reaching up to the sky, humbly bowing down or stretching out sideways.

Indulge yourself in some textures right down to the soft and tickly details.

Which colour combinations and subtle blends do you favour?

With care and asking, begin to gather shapely leaves, seedpods, petals, sticks, and such into the basket for your mandala. Invite Nature and Good Creator to co-create this art with you. Be sure to collect enough of one thing to make a pattern in a circle.

When you have collected at least seven different groupings of materials, find a flat clear space big enough to create your mandala, based on how many materials you gathered. Think of this space as your canvas or background colour.

Somewhere to the side, make individual piles for each different bunch of leaves, sticks, petals, seeds, cones, rocks or other ingredients you have gathered.

Begin in the center by making a shape to build on. You could place one rock in the center or several leaves radiating outward. It's up to you.

Have fun and play with this. Any loose material on the ground might be used to form into shapes. Do what you like.

Next add another layer radiating outward like a flower. Play with colour, texture and pattern.

Keep going around and around, layer by layer until you have completed your creation. If you need more embellishments, go find them.

When your mandala is complete, express your gratitude for this experience of creative play with Nature.

If you have a camera take some fun pictures.

Why not leave it as a love offering to Mother Earth?

Dismantling your mandala, if you wish, can be an important part of this creative activity. It gives you the opportunity to let go into a cycle of transformation. If you choose to take apart your mandala, do it with equal care and attention.

Just think what you'll do next time!

Another fun way to make a mandala is to draw, paint and collage with shapes such as a circle, spiral, heart, golden triangle, egg, whale tail, flower petal, crescent moon, leaves and many more. Give it a try and make one yourself. It's surprisingly simple to do!

Now that you have created a mandala using Nature's shapes, how about taking it to the next level to design your Sacred Garden? If you already have a garden, you can still benefit from this activity.

Nothing in the universe is separately "floating in space". It's all about good connections and flowing transitions.

Designing Your Sacred Garden Activity

Take a Leap and Dive In With Divine Hands

How about a stroll in your garden site? Bring your journal.

Look for a comfortable place to sit and write.

Take a few minutes to, you guessed it, get comfortable, quiet the mind, notice your body is breathing and has weight.

Ask Good Creator and Mother Nature to design this Sacred Garden with you and show you the way.

What will your garden be connected to? Acknowledge these connection and transition places such as, the house, a fence, pathways, the yard, trees or woods, neighbours.

Make these "imaginary" lines and divisions an integral and pleasing part of your design.

Look at the sunlight and imagine where the hot and cool spots will be throughout the day and season. It is important to learn where the sun will travel across your site as the seasons change.

Begin to envision a shape for the garden, or some connecting shapes within the garden. Look for any natural flowing lines in the land that give clues. Do you want to follow any of these or accent them?

Start drawing anything that comes to mind. Remember how the mandala began? You might want to begin with the center and work your way outward, but not necessarily.

Does the garden need a fence? What about a living fence or hedge with blackberries, roses or other wild shrubs? Think of all the life it could support. How can it be a beautiful part of your design?

Is there a possibility for different levels or terraces in the landscape?
Are there rocks you could work with creatively?

How will your paths move you through the garden with ease and grace? Can you imagine a pattern?

Look over your ingredients list in your journal. Can you envision where anything on your list, such as features and plants, might work well?

Consider areas to sit, play, create, or entertain.

You might want to lay out shapes in the garden with sticks or anything you can find. Let ideas flow without censoring them.

Take this creative process as far as you feel inspired to in the moment, and leave the rest for another time.

Trust that your Sacred Garden design is unfolding in perfect timing, and ideas, information, and resources are coming your way.

Once you begin working with the land, shaping a bed, moving rocks around, or building a fence, you will be shown, in some way, what to do next.

Get down in the dirt and dig it!

Message #8

What you need is given moment after moment.

My Story:

Many years ago, before I became a mother, I got the wild idea to create a labyrinth garden at the home I was renting. There was already a rectangular garden in place that I was tending. At first I couldn't imagine how I could do such a large and complicated design there.

Just a few hours after I had the vision, I visited a friend next door and noticed a book on her table that had several different labyrinths in it. I found one that was quite simple that appealed to me and held promise for my garden design.

I got busy laying out that labyrinth with sticks on the ground over the entire garden area. In order to fit the design, I needed to extend the fence about 10 feet into a bank of blackberry brambles. Not an appealing idea, I thought.

Soon after that, it occurred to me to call together a work bee for my birthday party to move the fence. People around here enjoy getting together to help tackle a big project and share a meal. The party was a great success! There was drumming and chocolate cheesecake, and more got accomplished than I thought possible.

The creation of that labyrinth garden was graced with magic, flow, inspiration and boundless energy.

Forming a Bed Activity

Define and Focus Energy

Making a bed creates a mini space to focus energy and give definition to the garden.

Once you have a basic idea of your garden design you can begin forming beds. This is a very exciting process. Ask for intuition and insight from the Divine and Nature.

What shapes and sizes of beds will you be working with and how are they going to connect and flow together?

How do you want to define your bed? By cultivating the soil and raking it into shape, placing rocks or wood around the edges, raising it slightly?

How will your pathways define your bed? Will they be grass, groundcovers, mulch or something else?

Consider how you will access the plants for tending or harvest. Make it easy to reach them. Think about how you will water the bed.

How is your soil? Is it primarily wet or dry? Will you need to bring in some better soil or work to improve the soil structure?

As you contemplate these factors work with the Earth to form your bed. Let it take shape. Work with the relaxed weight of your body instead of using force. Choose tools that will work best for the job.

As you begin forming a bed be receptive to your intuition and act on any insights that you get. Find your own rhythm and pace and honour it.

Take this process as far as you like, completing one bed or several. The next activity will be preparing the soil and planting the bed.

Give thanks for the blessings of this day.

Seventh Gate
Nurturing Your Garden with Beauty

Beauty above me
Beauty below me
Beauty all around me
Beauty before me
Beauty behind me
Beauty inside me

I love flowers. What gets you jazzed?

As you work in your Sacred Garden making beds, acquiring plants, forming pathways and adding embellishments, discover your own expression of beauty.

Your garden is loving you as muc

Everything that you actively care for and appreciate brightens up.

All the details count. If you see an eyesore, even a little one, do something with it. You will feel better and so will your garden.

s you are loving your garden!

Your garden is speaking to you all the time. Listen to it.

Preparing and Planting a Bed Activity

Co-Create with Nature

This activity may be done over a period of days as you find your own rhythm and creative flow. Remember to keep it simple, but give it your best.

Part I. Preparation

Start with one or two beds that you want to plant. Ask Good Creator and Nature for advice and assistance.

Take an impression of the bed or beds to be planted. Notice the shape, size, and exposure to the elements and relationship to the other beds.

Become familiar again with the soil by feeling it with your hands, smelling it, looking closely at it and digging into it.

What could you add to the soil to increase its vitality and support its loam? Possibly compost, rotted manure, a green manure crop, seaweed, ash, minerals, a biodynamic preparation or mulch?

Make use of good reference books if you need them.

Prepare the bed in your own loving way until you feel it is ready for planting or sowing. How's your enjoyment factor? Is there something you need? Are your tools working well for you? Work with the relaxed weight of your body and notice "body is breathing". Force is not needed. Let the relaxed weight and movement of the body do the work more efficiently.

Think of this bed as an expression of you and Nature creating together. Make it exciting. Try something new. Which plants do you want to create with in this bed? Each plant has its own unique beauty and expression. Think about all the colours, textures and characteristics you have discovered in the plants and how

they might intermix.

Consider the timing of flowering and harvest. How big are they likely to grow? How will you reach them for tending and harvest? Think about the angle the sunlight will be as the plants are growing.

Part II. Planting

Ask Good Creator and Nature to have a hand in this.

Have you ever planted by following the cycles of the moon? What I have learned is when the full moon shines bright the energies are at their peak in the upper parts of the plants. Then as the moon wanes, the energies begin their descent to the roots. In general, it is good to plant crops that produce above the ground during the waxing moon and plant root crops during the waning moon cycle. Do your own experimenting and observing to see what works well. If you want to get really cosmic tune into the sun, moon and stars!

When the time has come to sow or plant, gather your seeds, plants or bulbs together. By the way, how's the weather? Are you aware of the elements?

As you begin to arrange the plants on the bed or draw lines in the soil to mark the sowing pattern, however you set it up, let all that you have learned so far inform your design.

Be open to intuition and act on any insights you get.

I recently learned an inspiring sowing practice: Before you sow your seeds, place a few seeds under your tongue for at least nine minutes. Use only untreated seeds for this. Then hold the seed between the palms of your hands for about half a minute while standing barefoot where you will be sowing the seed. Then blow on the seed lightly warming it with your breath and with open hands present the seed to the celestial bodies for thirty seconds. Wait three days after sowing these seeds before you water them in. From this process the seeds will know everything that is within you, and will provide for you the best nutrition and medicine for your well being. For more information on this subject read the book "Anastasia" listed in the back of this book.

When you nestle your plants and seeds into the ground, use gentleness and firmness. Sing or talk to them. Tell them how big, beautiful or tasty they are going to be.

Send them your blessings when you water them in.

Give your thanks and praise.

Message #9

When things are in their right place they are beautiful.

Trees are treasures we can offer to our next generation. They gift us with serenity, beauty, strength, shelter, fruits and nuts, clean air, soil and water protection, microclimates, homes for wildlife, playgrounds, gorgeous wood and much more.

Imagine the Earth with an abundance of magnificent trees!

Planting a Tree for the Children Activity

Take Action to Create an Abundant Future

Trees are magical.

The more you get to know a tree, spend time with it and give to it, the more you realize how much it is giving back. This mutual support can go on for generations.

What kind of trees do you like?

Part I. Choosing Your Tree

Write about your favourite trees in your journal. Think about trees that you loved as a child as well as the ones you love now. Connect with your heart and remember your feelings.

What kind of tree would you like to plant? Imagine what it will look like in a hundred years. Who will be enjoying it?

Where might you plant your tree? Consider how far the roots can grow and what it will shade as it matures. How much sun will it need at its early stages and at maturity in order for it to thrive? Ask the Divine for inspiration and let Nature inform you.

Find out if the conditions are right for that tree where you want to plant it. Ask for and receive guidance.

Consider choosing a hardy variety that you can rely on, one that has been around for a long time.

When you have decided what kind of tree you are going to plant, the next step is to find your special seed or young seedling. Some possibilities are to gather the seed or seedling yourself, find it through a friend or neighbour, or purchase it from a nursery or seed catalogue.

Find out the optimal time of year for planting trees in your area.

Part II. Planting

Once you have your seed or seedling, carefully decide where and when you will plant it. Ask Good Creator and Nature for ideas. Use your imagination to see it in the future looking radiant.

If you don't have your spot picked out, sow a seed in a pot on the windowsill to plant later. The idea is to have this little tree in a place where you can befriend and care for it. Then you can discover the right place for it to thrive.

How about inviting a child to participate? They can be quite intuitive and connected.

When you are ready, prepare the soil for your tree. Take your time and be receptive in the process. Give it just the right conditions to grow, as best you can.

See if you can be active and receptive at the same time while you are handling the seed or seedling and putting it in the soil.

Give it your blessing as you water it in and imagine it thriving.

Fantastic! You have just given the next generation the promise of a magical tree.

Eighth Gate

The Balance of Nature

Earth, Air, Fire
and Water
Great Mystery
Forming and transforming
In perfect unity
Moment by moment.

Balance and harmony are already here. How could we be more receptive to this law? One way is to be aware of the elements Earth, Air, Fire and Water.

The balance of Nature includes the balance of these elements in and around us.

As you continue co-creating your Sacred Garden, contemplate the balance and harmony of these elements. Ask Good Creator and Nature to reveal them to you while you are working with the soil, tending the plants, watering and enjoying the sunshine. Use your insights to adjust, for example, how and when you water your garden or how you might improve the soil.

These next activities will help you to get started.

Meeting Earth, Air, Fire and Water Activity

Cultivate New Awareness

These elements are in us and in the garden. It's good to let our conditioned ideas and definitions take a back seat while we open to Mystery. Let your own experience teach you. Spread this activity over a few days, picking one element at a time. The order is up to you.

WATER

Choose a special glass and fill it with good drinking Water. Bring it and your journal with you into the garden.

Find a comfortable place to sit where you can be close to the soil.

Hold the glass of Water in your hands as you say in your own words "Good Creator I wish to learn something new about Water and its effect on the garden and myself."

Give thanks for the Water and all that it gives.

Give the Water your blessing and ask that it thrive in your garden.

With gratitude drink a few sips of the Water while being especially receptive to its properties. Taste it and feel it in your body.

Pour some Water on the soil and attentively watch how it moves and interacts with the ground. Where does it go?

Ask if there is a Water message for you. Write down anything that comes to mind and things that you notice that seem interesting.

When you feel complete with this exchange, give thanks.

My Water message:

The river is flowing, flowing and growing,
the river is flowing, down to the sea.

FIRE

Want to build a fire circle in your Sacred Garden? This activity must be done when there are no fire bans in your area. The fire can be quite small if needed.

Gather some paper, a few pieces of dry wood, matches, and a trowel or shovel. Do you have any special rocks that you would like to use around the circle? You will need some rocks either from the garden or somewhere else. If you have a smudge stick of sage, cedar, rosemary or some resin to burn, bring it. Bring along your journal.

Walk out to the garden and say in your own words, "Good Creator I wish to learn something new about Fire."

Ask where in the garden would be the best place for a Fire circle. Usually your first impulse is right.

Begin by clearing and digging out a circle for the pit. It can be any size but keep it simple for now.

Look for rocks to go around the pit and always ask permission in your own way before you use them.

Begin placing the rocks around the circle. You could start with the four directions, north, south, east and west, or any other way you like. Make it your own fun and creative ceremonial expression.

When the outer circle is complete, begin layering up the inside with the paper, kindling and wood, gathering sticks or leaves as needed. You are layering up your prayer.

As you light the Fire ask for the gift of cleansing and purification on the garden and yourself. Offer up any other prayers you have at this time. If you have any sage, cedar, rosemary, pine resin or other, light them now for purification.

Pay attention to the signs of what is happening around you.

Give thanks for the Fire as you blow on it and fan it. Avoid breathing in the smoke. Watch and listen to the Fire as it burns. When the Fire has burnt out, notice the miracle of transformation that has just occurred.

Take some of the ash and spread it around the garden giving thanks for its nourishment to the soil.

Ask if there is a Fire message for you.

Write about your experience.

AIR

Ah, a breath of fresh Air would be nice. A light breezy day is good for this activity.

Another reason to pick up your journal and head out to your garden.

Stand in your garden and say in your own words, “Good Creator, I wish to learn something new about Air.”

Begin walking around the garden noticing the weight of your body on the ground. Notice your body is breathing. No hurry, no pause. Feel the Air entering your body.

Feel the Air touching your skin.

Is there anything flying through the Air? Take an impression of the movement. Look for seeds that you can toss up and watch glide through the Air.

See how the Air moves across the plants and animates them. If there is no breeze then use your breath to blow the Air. Listen to any sounds of Air moving.

What qualities are you noticing about Air?

When you feel ready to finish up, give thanks for the Air and ask if there are any messages for you.

Write your experience in your journal.

My Air message:

Air is the great carrier.

EARTH

Have you ever created an Earth altar? Children love this activity.

Bring with you to the garden a candle in a protective holder, matches, your best incense if you like, a gathering basket, and your journal.

Say in your own words, "Good Creator, I wish to learn something new about Earth."

Ask where would be the best spot to make an Earth altar on the ground. Wherever you feel drawn to do it will be good.

Begin gathering interesting things from the Earth for your altar such as flowers, seedpods, rocks, shells, feathers, and sticks. Ask for inspiration and permission on what to gather and look closely.

Begin decorating your altar space with the material you have gathered. Use your imagination and care, honouring the Earth with her beauty.

Set up the candle and incense within your earthy creation. When you are ready, light the candle remembering Fire, and the incense remembering Air, as you express your gratitude to the Earth.

Find a comfortable position to watch, listen and enjoy the moment.

Ask for an Earth message.

Write about your experience in your journal.

My Earth message:
Love all the Earth.

Message #10

Everything is included.

NINTH GATE

Celebration Ceremony & Rest

Is it celebration time yet?

You and Nature have done such good work together and things are shaping up. What was it that you made this garden for?

Relax and take your shoes off.

Your Sacred Garden is like a megaphone to the Universe.
What do you want to say?

Give thanks and praise with your garden everyday.

Bask in the moonlight
and gaze at the stars.

Creating a Simple Ceremony Activity

Take Quality Time to Honour and Celebrate

Here is your opportunity to further acknowledge and honour the co-creative work that you, Good Creator and Nature have done in your Sacred Garden. It is a time to give thanks for the gifts given and received.

Think of a theme for your ceremony, such as harvest, fall equinox, your birthday or anything that is truly meaningful to you. Ask Good Creator for ideas and inspiration.

Do you want to invite anyone to participate?

Consider if you would like to have singing, drumming, or some type of music.

How about creating an altar with a few meaningful objects like a candle, silk cloth, a flower arrangement, seeds and fruits from the garden, a chalice for water or wine. Remember to nurture it with beauty.

Where in the garden would you like to set it up? Will you share some food or drink?

What do you want to express during this special time?

Write out a simple plan for your ceremony and allow for some spontaneity. Create something that is beautiful, meaningful, and works well for you. Keep it simple and enjoyable.

Choose your date and go for it. Have fun and celebrate the life that is gathering in your Sacred Garden.

Take a few photographs if you have a camera, and be sure to write about your experience.

Message #11

Being conscious is celebrating Life.

Many beings that most people don't see inhabit Nature and do their work in the garden just as we do. It is good to acknowledge and honour their presence in some way.

Creating a Fairy House Activity

Honour the "Unseen" Helpers

This is an imaginative activity to do with children or with your childlike self. These are for the "good fairies" and other "unseen" helpers you have in your garden.

Go around your garden and look for a spot that you imagine a fairy would want to visit.

Smooth out the ground just a bit so you can create a special little space.

Go around the garden gently gathering little flowers or petals, interesting seedpods, feathers, moss, sticks, anything that looks inviting.

Create little beds, tables, rooms, and whatever comes to mind. Your child friend will have lots of ideas.

Make it inviting, cozy and beautiful. Keep decorating until it looks and feels finished. Is there anything else you would like to add? Ask the fairies what they like.

When you are finished, offer it to the good fairies and unseen helpers. Watch what happens over the next few days.

Wasn't that fun? Take a photo if you like.

Make a fairy house when you need a break from the normal routine or when a child shows up looking for something to do.

Encourage children to play in your garden and have tea parties.

You are well on your way with your Sacred Garden.

Continue to work with your Guiding Light and all that you have learned. More will come.

As the seasons cycle round, the spiral of wisdom deepens. Your garden will teach you what you need to know day by day, moment by moment.

Every moment
new life is given.

Inherent in every natural cycle
is the time for rest and integration.

Nighttime, winter and stillness...
the place of the unmanifested
potential.

Let yourself and your garden have
this sacred and potent time of rest.

Just around the corner awaits the
promise of spring, with alive
beginnings, fresh awareness, and
the miracle of birth.

The Universe is singing
on a warm and silent breeze
for you to dance
with the Beloved
in the Love
Light and Beauty
of your Sacred Garden.

Message #12

Life is supporting life always and everywhere.

Acknowledgements

My greatest thanks goes to Good Creator for giving me Life eternal.
Thank you to Mother Earth and Nature for supporting and nurturing this Life.
Thank you to my loving, supportive and generous mother and father for all your help along the way.
Thank you to my daughter Angelica for being so patient and loving while I spent many long hours on the computer.
Thank you to my first gardening teachers: David Buckner with the Linnaea Farm Ecological Gardening Programme, and Nori Fletcher with the Hollyhock Foundation garden.
Thank you to my first gardening partner Alex Hornby who taught me so much about herbal medicine and shared my passion for flowers and nature intelligences.
Thank you to The Breema Center for teaching me the art of being present, the essence of harmonious life, the nurturing and nourishing Breema® bodywork and Self-Breema excercises and for helping me to be real.
Thank you to my drumming teachers Babatunde Olatunji, Gordy and Zoe Ryan and Mamady Keita for teaching me the rhythms of life and keeping me in the beat.
Thank you to Dorothy Maclean and Machalle Small Wright for introducing me to communicating with the devas and nature spirits and for all your co-creative work with Nature.
Thank you to Caz Ratcliff and Pamela Boles for teaching me the art of flower arranging.
Thank you to Gavin Livingstone for all your support while writing this book, for introducing me to the "Gratitude" and "Knock Three Times" activities, and for getting me out into Nature more.
Thank you to Ron Bazaar for inspiring me to write this book and for all of your help with the editing.
Thank you to Lorna Brown for your expertise, encouragement and words of wisdom.
Thank you to Richard Trueman for so generously teaching me about digital photography and computers.
Thank you to Suzan Denis for keeping an eye on the integrity of the design.
Thank you to Ester Strijbos for teaching me how to design with text in InDesign.
Thank you to all of my dear friends who gave their honest input and support to help polish the book.
Thank you to Anastasia and Vladmir Merge for inspiring me with your vision and hope for the world.
Thank you to all of the unseen helpers who wove their magic into this project.
And last but not least, thank you to the flowers for nurturing my soul.

Further Reading

Breema and the Nine Principles of Harmony
Every Moment Is Eternal: The Timeless Wisdom of Breema
Freedom Is In This Moment: 365 Insights for Daily Life
Self-Breema: Exercises for Harmonious Life
by Jon Schreiber, D.C. Breema Center Publishing www.breema.com

Roots Shoots Buckets and Boots: Gardening Together with Children
by Sharon Lovejoy Workman Publishing, New York

The Road Back to Nature: Regaining the Paradise Lost
The Natural Way of Farming: The Theory and Practice of Green Philosophy
by Masanobu Fukuoka Japan Publications Inc. Tokyo and New York

A Year On the Gardening Path: A 52 Week Organic Gardening Guide
by Carolyn Herriot New Society Publishers www.newsociety.com

Rodale's All-New Encyclopedia of Organic Gardening
by Fern Marshall Bradley and Barbara W. Ellis Rodale Press

Gardening When It Counts by Steve Solomon New Society Publishers

Mycelium Running: How Mushrooms Can Help Save the World
by Paul Satmets Ten Speed Press www.tenspeed.com

How To Make a Forest Garden: A Do It Yourself Guide to A New Way of Gardening by Patrick Whitefield Permanent Publications, UK
Chelsea Green Publishing, VT, USA

Anastasia Book 1 (also recommended Books 2 - 8.2) of the Ringing Cedars Series by Vladimir Megre Ringing Cedars Press www.ringingcedars.com

The Healing Power of Water
by Masaru Emoto Hay House Inc. www.hayhouse.com

Creating Sacred Space with Feng Shui
by Karen Kingston Broadway Books, New York

Behaving As If the God In All Life Mattered
Perelandra Garden Workbook (I & II): A Complete Guide To Gardening with Nature Intelligences
(and other books) by Machaelle Small Wright www.perelandra-ltd.com

To Hear the Angels Sing: An Odyssey of Co-Creation with the Devic Kingdom
To Honor the Earth: Reflections on Living in Harmony with Nature
by Dorothy Maclean

Ask and It Is Given: Learning to Manifest Your Desires
by Esther and Jerry Hicks Hay House, Inc. www.hayhouse.com

Credits

Photographs taken in the Hollyhock Foundation garden include pages: 12, 20, 24, 26, 28, 31, 32, 33, 35, 44, 59, 60, 62, 73, 74, 79, 93, 94, 97, 102, 103, 104, 105, 113, 118, 131, 132, 137, 143, 144, & 148.
www.hollyhock.ca

The Linnaea Farm Land Trust on Cortes Island offers an eight month ecological gardening programme that engages the heart, mind and hands in the theory and practice of organic food production, permaculture design and sustainable farming skills. As a graduate of this programme, I highly recommend it.

Linnaea Farm
Ecological Garden Programme
Box 98
Manson's Landing, BC Canada V0P 1K0
phone 250 935-6717
www.linnaeafarm.org email:info@linnaeafarm.org

Library and Archives Canada Cataloguing in Publication

Raaen, Claudia, 1962
The art of sacred gardening : creating beauty and abundance in harmony with nature / Claudia Raaen.
1. Gardening--Religious aspects. 2. Gardens--Religious aspects.
3. Spiritual life. I. Title.

SB454.R32 2008 635.01 C2008-907390-8

Published by
Sacred Gardening
Box 134
Manson's Landing, BC V0P 1K0
Canada

www.sacredgardening.com

ISBN 978-0-9811150-0-9

Printed in Canada
[illegible] FSC paper